STEP-by-STEP

GEOGRAPHY

Weather

Paul Humphrey

Illustrated by Roger Stewart
and Shirley Tourret

Ⓟ CHILDREN'S PRESS®

A Division of Grolier Publishing

LONDON • NEW YORK • HONG KONG • SYDNEY
DANBURY, CONNECTICUT

© 1996 Franklin Watts

First American Edition 1997 by

Children's Press

A Division of Grolier Publishing

Sherman Turnpike

Danbury, CT 06816

ISBN: 0 516 20238 3

Library of Congress Cataloging-in-Publication Data

Humphrey, Paul, 1952-

The Weather/Paul Humphrey; illustrated by Roger Stewart and Shirley Tourret

p cm -- (Step-by-step geography)

Includes index.

Summary: Explores all kinds of weather phenomena, including sun, rain, wind, hurricanes, tornadoes, and snow.

1. Weather--juvenile literature. 2. Meteorology--juvenile literature. I. Stewart, Roger, ill.

II. Tourret, Shirley, ill. III. Title. IV. Series: Step-by-step (Elgin, Ill.)

QC981.3.H86 1997

551.5--dc20   96-18103

CIP AC

Printed in Dubai

Planning and production by The Creative Publishing Company

Designed by Ian Winton

Edited by Patience Coster

Consultant: Keith Lye

Photographs: Bruce Coleman: page 5, top (Gunter Ziesler), 7 (Dr Eckart Pott),

9 (Erwin and Peggy Bauer), 14, top (Hans Reinhard), 16 (Kim Taylor), 25 (Luiz Claudio Marigo),

31 (Steve Alden); Frank Lane Picture Agency: page 5 (C Carvalho), 17 (Frants Hartmann); Oxford Scientific Films: cover and page 13 (Warren Faidley), page 14

(Stan Osolinski); Science Photo Library: page 29 (NASA/SPL); Tony Stone Worldwide: page 6 (Andy Sacks), 12 (Ken Biggs),

20 (Ralph Wetmore), 26 (Alan Puzey), 27 (Yvette Cardozo), 28 (Arnulf Husmo).

Contents

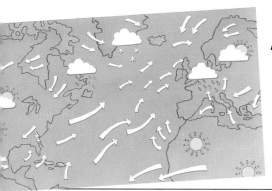

Weather Everywhere

What's the weather like today? Is it warm and sunny, or windy and rainy? Was it foggy this morning, or was there a sharp frost? Perhaps there is snow on the ground.

Have you noticed how the weather changes at different times of the year? It is usually much colder in the winter than it is in the spring and summer.

The weather is also different in different places. In some places, like Africa, it is warm all the time.

In others, like Antarctica, it is cold all the time.

5

Sunny Weather

Most of us like sunny weather. On sunny days, we can go to the beach or out for a picnic. Farmers like the sun in summer because it helps their crops to ripen.

But too much sun can be harmful. Long periods of **drought** can kill crops. Then people and animals may have nothing to eat and face starvation.

Rainy Weather

Plants, animals, and people all need the rain. Without water, we would die. But do you know where rain comes from?

Have you ever watched a kettle boiling? The water in the kettle turns to steam, or **water vapor**, when it is heated. If the steam hits a cold wall or window, it turns back into water again.

Rain is formed in almost the same way. Look at the picture below.

2 These clouds are blown on to the land. When they reach the mountains, they rise upward with the wind. The clouds grow in size and raindrops are formed.

1 Water from the sea is heated by the sun. Air containing water vapor rises and cools. The water vapor is turned into clouds.

◄ Rainbows are formed when the sun shines through tiny drops of rain. To see a rainbow you should stand with your back to the sun. The rain must be falling somewhere in front of you.

MAKE A RAINBOW!

1 Choose a fine, sunny day.
2 Fill a plant sprayer with water, or ask if you can borrow the garden hose.
3 Squirt the water so that it makes a mist in the sunlight.
4 To see a rainbow, move slowly making sure that the sun is behind you.

3 The rain falls on to the hills, finding its way into streams and rivers and then back to the sea again. This process is known as the water cycle.

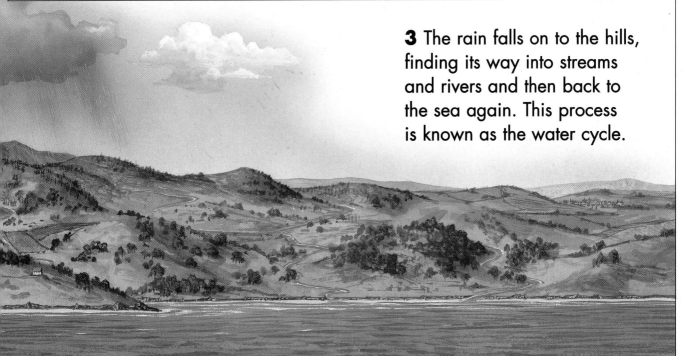

Windy Weather

Windy weather is good for flying
a kite and for sailing.

Look at this map. It shows some of the **global** winds that
blow across the Earth.

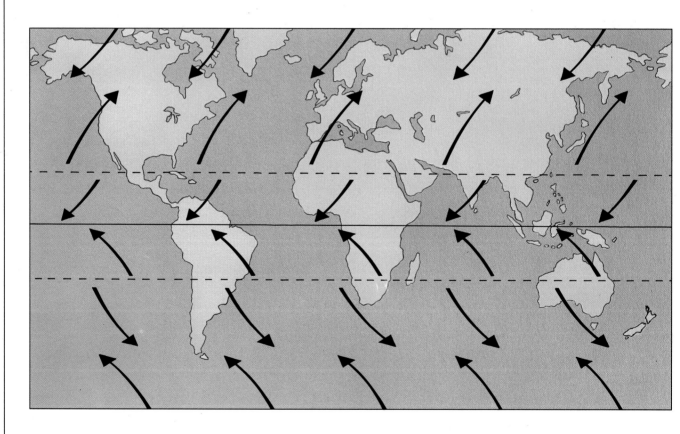

Sea Breezes

Near to the coast there are local winds, called sea breezes.

During the daytime, the sea breeze blows from the sea on to the land.

At night, the breeze blows from the land on to the sea.

MAKE A WIND VANE

1 Take a drinking straw and make a short cut lengthways in each end. Cut a pointed fish head and tail from some coloured card and push into the ends of the straw.

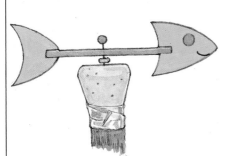

2 Fix a cork with sticky tape to one end of a garden cane. Ask an adult to push a pin through the balance point of the straw, then through a bead and into the cork. Take the wind vane into the open and push it into the soil.

3 Ask an adult to show you where north is and mark with an N on the cork. Mark south, west and east in the same way. The wind vane will point in the direction that the wind is blowing from.

Hurricanes and Tornadoes

In the **tropical** regions of the earth, near to the **equator**, there are violent winds called hurricanes. They can destroy whole towns and cities.

The fiercest winds of all occur in tornadoes. A tornado is a spinning funnel of air. It moves along the ground sucking up anything in its way, like a giant vacuum cleaner.

Many tornadoes are found in the central United States.

The Worst Tornado

Although tornadoes occur most often in the United States, the worst tornado in history swept through Bangladesh on April 26th, 1989. The town of Shaturia was destroyed and more than 1,000 people were killed. Survivors say they saw houses being blown away like pieces of paper. At least 30,000 people were left without homes as a result of the tornado.

Frost and Ice

Have you ever been out on a cold winter morning when the trees are covered with glistening frost? Frost is formed when moisture in the air freezes in very cold weather. Where the moist air touches branches of trees or blades of grass, tiny ice **crystals** are formed.

During very cold weather the water in puddles, ponds, and lakes also freezes into ice. In very cold places whole lakes and even the sea can freeze over in winter.

The Rock Breaker

Frost can even shatter mountain rocks. Rain collects in cracks in the rocks. When it freezes, it gets bigger and the rock breaks open.

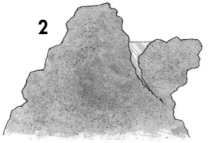

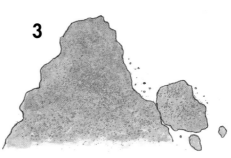

WHAT HAPPENS TO WATER WHEN IT FREEZES?

1 Fill a plastic bottle with water. Screw on the top.

2 Put the bottle in the freezer for the night.

3 In the morning, take the bottle out of the freezer.

4 You will find that either the bottle has cracked or the top has popped off. This is because water expands, or gets bigger, when it freezes.

Snow

Most of us like the snow. Snow is great for sledding and making snowmen, but it makes life difficult for farmers. Sometimes their animals get stuck in deep drifts or are stranded without food.

Snowflakes are formed when the air inside a cloud is very cold. The droplets of liquid in the air freeze and then fall as snow. No two snowflakes are alike, but they all have six sides.

Tropical Snow

Did you know that there is even snow in very hot countries? The top of Mount Kilimanjaro in Tanzania, Africa, is always covered in snow even though it is hot at the bottom of the mountain. This is because it gets colder the higher you go, so high mountaintops are always cold places.

Clouds

Different types of clouds suggest different kinds of weather. Look at the picture.

Cirrus

Cirrus clouds are the thin, wispy, white clouds you often see on dry days. They usually mean that the weather is going to change.

Altocumulus

Cumulus

Cirrus clouds are often followed by small masses of fluffy altocumulus clouds. Tall masses of altocumulus may mean that a storm is on its way.

Cumulus clouds are the white, flu clouds you see on fine summer c

Stratus clouds form as a low sheet and may cause fog over hills.

Stratus

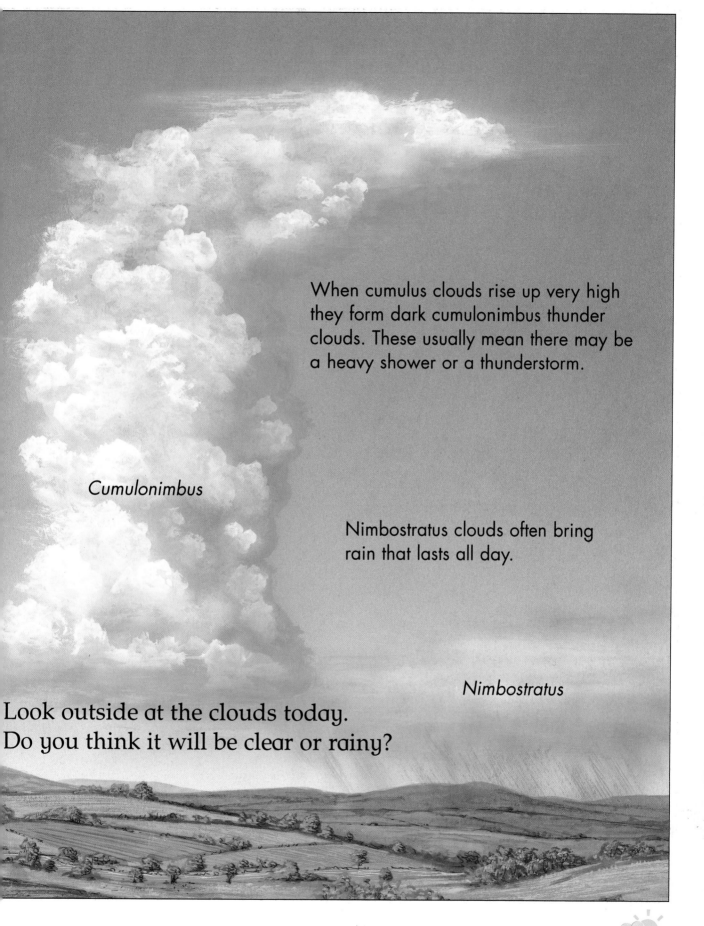

When cumulus clouds rise up very high they form dark cumulonimbus thunder clouds. These usually mean there may be a heavy shower or a thunderstorm.

Cumulonimbus

Nimbostratus clouds often bring rain that lasts all day.

Nimbostratus

Look outside at the clouds today.
Do you think it will be clear or rainy?

Thunder and Lightning

Do you like the crashing and flashing of thunder and lightning? Thunderstorms occur when the air is very damp. Huge cumulonimbus clouds form and tower high into the sky.

Lightning Strike

Lightning hardly ever strikes in the same place twice. However, very tall buildings can be hit many times. The Empire State Building in New York City was struck by lightning 48 times in a single day.

The flash of lightning that you see is a giant electric spark leaping from the cloud to the ground. The thunder that you hear is the noise made by hot air along the path of the lightning that expands very quickly.

Climate

Climate means the sort of weather that is usual for a certain area over many years.

In many tropical regions near to the equator it is hot and wet all year round. Near to the North and South Poles it is very cold all the year round.

Regions with a desert climate have very little rain.

In between the poles and the tropics is the **temperate** region. Here the weather is usually mild.

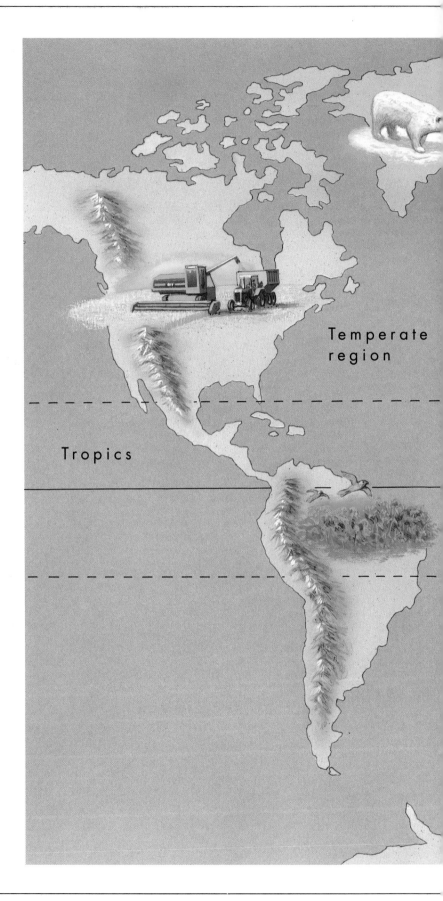

Temperate region

Tropics

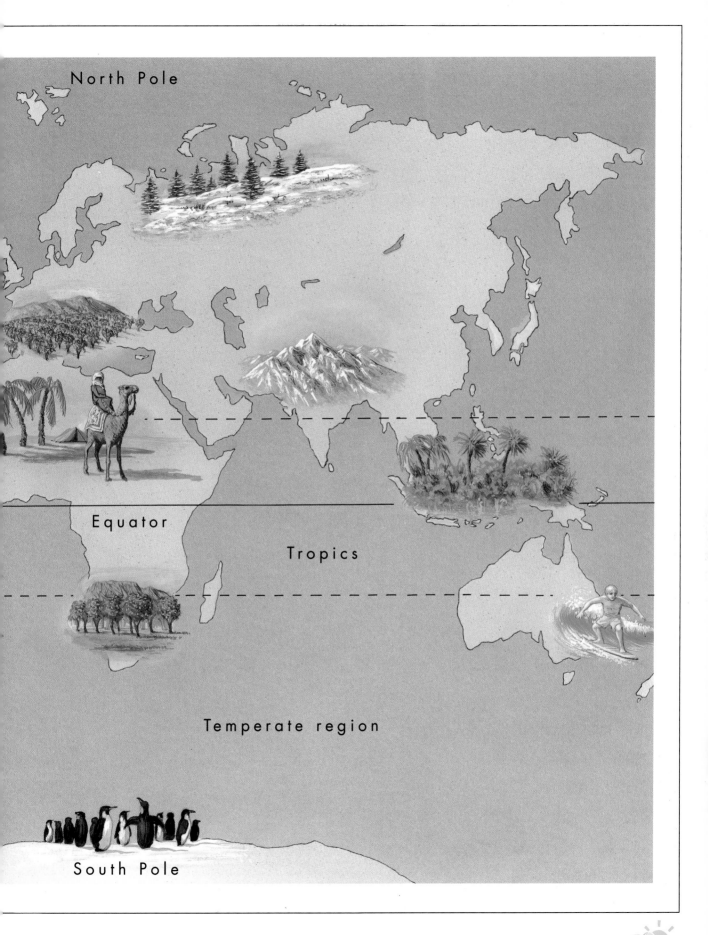

North Pole

Equator

Tropics

Temperate region

South Pole

Seasons

In the temperate regions of the world, there are four seasons — spring, summer, autumn, and winter. Which is your favorite season?

The northern and southern **hemispheres** of the earth have their seasons at opposite times of the year. When it is summer in Europe and North America, it is winter in South Africa and Australia.

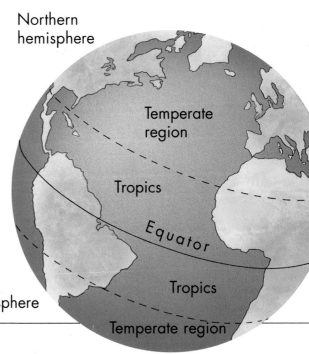

Northern hemisphere

Temperate region

Tropics

Equator

Tropics

Southern hemisphere

Temperate region

Rainy Season

This picture shows the rainy season in the tropics. In the tropical regions of the earth, it is hot all the time and there are often just three seasons — the hot season, the dry season, and the rainy season.

Weather, Climate, and People

You probably wear different clothes in the summer and in the winter. In summer you might wear thin T-shirts and shorts. In winter, you'll need thicker sweaters, coats, and boots.

In very hot countries, people wear loose cotton clothes, or very few clothes at all. Old houses were built with thick walls and small windows to keep out the sun's heat. Now, many houses in hot countries have **air-conditioning** to keep them cool.

In cold countries people wear many layers of wool clothes and furs to keep themselves warm. Their homes are **insulated** to keep in as much heat as possible. This Inuit man has built an igloo, a house made of blocks of snow.

Weather Forecasts

Weather forecasts tell us what we can expect the weather to be like. They are useful if you are planning a picnic or a day out at the beach. Airline pilots and ships' captains need to know what kind of weather they are traveling into.

There are thousands of weather stations around the world. They help **meteorologists** to figure out what tomorrow's weather will be.

Meteorologists also use computers and satellites, like this one, to make their weather forecasts.

TV weather forecasters use charts and symbols to show us what kind of weather we can expect.

The Changing Weather

Weather and climate are changing all the time. Two million years ago there was an Ice Age, and much of North America and Europe lay under a sheet of ice all the year round.

The climate could change again in the future. How do you think life where you live would change if the climate became much warmer or much colder?

Global Warming

The dust and smoke from large volcanoes can blot out the sun and change the weather for a time. The smoke from chimneys and car exhausts is also affecting the climate across the whole world. This change in climate is known as global warming.

Glossary

Air-conditioning: A system for cleaning air and controlling its temperature before it enters a room or a building

Crystal: A three-dimensional form of a solidified substance. Ice crystals are made from frozen water

Drought: Lack of rain

Equator: An imaginary line around the earth, dividing it into northern and southern hemispheres

Global: Affecting the whole earth

Hemisphere: Half of the earth

Insulated: Lined with protective material to keep the heat in

Meteorologist: A person who studies and forecasts the weather

Temperate: A climate that is neither very hot nor very cold

Tropical: The hot, wet climate that exists in the tropics (the two imaginary lines around the earth on either side of the equator)

Water vapor: Invisible moisture in the air

Index